A

SURVIVAL GUIDE FOR THE OVER- THE-ROAD TRUCK DRIVER

What you Should Know
BUT were Never Told

I DEDICATE THIS BOOK TO:

My wife Heather and my daughter Grace, for without their patience, support and sacrifice, this book would have never been possible

My Mom, who taught me to flap my wings and fly

My Pop, who taught me work ethic and how to be a man. You are missed every day

My grandparents, who were proud of everything I did

My English Humanities teacher, Pamela Vaughn, who helped me discover my talent for writing

TABLE OF CONTENTS

INTRODUCTION

Welcome to Trucking

For almost 100 years, trucking has seen many changes, both good and bad; depending on whom you talk to. One constant, however, remains the same – the need for trucks and those who drive them. **WITHOUT TRUCKS AMERICA STOPS!** Although that sounds like a cliché, it is an in your face fact and has been true for the past 40 or so years. This year alone forecasters predict a driver shortage of roughly 200,000 drivers. With the thousands of companies rolling across our highways, truck drivers have many companies to pick from and some of them will give you empty promises and you will be guaranteed just four things: To have a position that is the most underpaid, overworked, over regulated and time restricted occupation in the country.

I hope, as you thumb through this Guide, it opens your eyes to things you did not know before or it will help you see the things you forgot or did not know about. Albeit, these are my own experiences and mishaps, I guarantee you will or already have experienced them and maybe, just maybe, I can help you get along a little easier. My whole intent of this Guide is to help those who have never driven before, those in need of a refresher course, and for those who just want a good read about the trucking industry. This is a book written by a trucker for truckers; entry level and seasoned.

Welcome to Trucking!!

FORWARD

The American Trucker

There are two types of truck drivers – those who drive to live and those who live to drive. To the first type of driver, driving a truck is a job – just that – a job involving a daily routine that entails getting up early in the morning, driving that big beast around town, stopping for deliveries here and there and returning back to the yard. There is nothing in it for that type of driver but a paycheck, a weekend off, and doing the same thing over again day after day just to pay the bills. It becomes a daily chore and if given a choice, they would move on to the next job if they become bored or just wanted out.

Now the second type of truck driver is an entirely different breed and honestly, a dying one. I, myself, am lumped into this category. We have a passion – something that flows through our veins that we cannot explain. We were born with it; it's in our genes. Maybe it started when we first drove the tractor on the farm or when we got our license for the very first time. It's really hard to describe. It's a true calling. There is just something about turning that key, hearing the rumble of the motor, the shifting of gears and the open road. It even gets to the point when the longer we don't do it, the greater the passion. It's a drive unlike any other; we were made for this. We are the Knights of the Road. We keep America moving. We are the American Trucker.

CHAPTER ONE

The Lonely Road - How to Cope

One of the most difficult things to learn in trucking is how to cope with the "lonely road." It is an acquired talent and also one of the main contributing factors of drivers leaving the industry. Plainly, this is where the strong survive and the weak perish. One must be able to get a grasp on the separation anxiety all drivers experience when they enter this field.

It has been the fourteen years of driving experience, at the time I started writing this book, which has enabled me to get used to being on the road away from loved ones and my home. When it does start getting to me and becomes burdensome, I have discovered ways to overcome it. It also happens that I have been given the opportunity to drive for a company which does not send me out on the road for weeks at a time; if they do, it is not very often.

Most of you reading this book work for companies that keep you out for weeks at a time so this will come in handy for you.

The following is a small list of helpful hints and suggestions to help eliminate the boredom and routine on the open road.

- **Have a supportive spouse or significant other**

  The first and foremost important factor of realizing a career in trucking is to have the backing of a supportive partner. Having this person at home to talk to, or even to vent, about your day, helps to relieve the stress of being away from home out here on your own.

  Many drivers make the mistake of entering this industry on a whim with no notice to their partner and all they succeed to do is fail; usually owing thousands of dollars in truck school loans and wasting a whole lot of people's time. My advice to all the potential "newbies" to this industry who decide they want to start driving truck? **Think** before you commit. If you have an established home and partner just don't jump into it; discuss it with him/her. This decision affects all those around you in your immediate life.

Before I met my wife, I had 8 years on the road and we dated every now and then. It was a silent understanding that this is what I do and it is a part of who I am; it's a package deal. I really didn't think much about it because things were not all that serious yet and it was just me that I had to worry about. We have been together for 7 years, as of the start of this book in 2008, and it is because of her support that I am able to stay in the seat. Without it, I would have to hang up my keys. However, I am the minority of drivers. Most drivers **are** single and that is when this career works well. In fact, most single drivers live in their trucks so all they have to do is drive and not have to worry about the day to day family commitments.

- **Cell Phone**

As much of a pain in the ass they can be, cellphones are just as much of an important tool as the seat you are sitting in. When it seems to get really bad and you can't deal with things anymore, home is just a push of a button away. You'll be amazed just how much better you'll feel when you can hear a familiar voice on the other end. Cell phones are your lifeline should you have a breakdown, get sick, have an accident, etc.

When you do decide to get a cell phone (believe me, there are those out there who still don't have one) just be sure the coverage is decent. I currently use Verizon and as far as I'm concerned, it has the best service out there. The most important factor in deciding which cell phone provider you will use is the coverage in desolate areas, e.g., Nevada, Wyoming, western Texas, New Mexico, et. al. Be sure to check the roaming rates and/or night and weekend charges. If you get a plan that does not give you free, unlimited hours on any of these, you are in for a huge sticker shock. It seems to be the norm today that all roaming and night/weekend charges are included so you really can't go wrong; Verizon includes all of these. Do research and you will get the best deal. There are a few carriers that actually give trucker discounts. Do your homework.

- **Sirius-XM Satellite Radio**

I got my first radio in 2005 when there was total hype about Howard Stern coming over to the space-waves. I had been an occasional listener of his on "terrestrial" radio and thought how cool it would be to hear his show the way it should have been. I was right; it's a pretty good radio show. However, I began to listen to the other 100+ channels and I gotta tell ya, there is everything on there. Any music, from every genre, to every football game and all kinds of entertainment shows. The best part of this subscription is the news, weather and traffic. It has come in very handy for me as I drive all over the country.   The best part – it's tax deductible!!

CHAPTER TWO

Home-Time

One, if not the single-most, factor, of truck driving is the home-time you are supposed to get – or at least you were promised to get. The first question to ask any potential company that wants to hire you is how long will I be out, when will I get home and for how much time I will have at home.

Many drivers jump at the first company that will hire them, and then two months later, when they are 3000 miles away from home, they ask about home-time; not the prime time for this question. This is one of the reasons for truck abandonment; which is not a good idea. This will not only hurt your credit, it will also prevent you from being hired by another company. Once this is on your record it cannot be removed. My advice to you is to investigate and research any and all job opportunities.

Never settle for the first one you contact unless, in the end, they are the carrier with the best package. Some companies guarantee home-time while others "promise" it and usually don't deliver. If you can (Good Luck) get their "promises" in writing. You may use it against them down the road if need be.

Another factor when considering a carrier is the location of their terminals in relation to where you live; if it is a concern. For instance, if you live in Fargo, North Dakota and you go to work for a carrier in St. Louis, Missouri, chances are you won't be going home too often as you do not live in a major freight lane. As of late, most carriers will only hire within a 50 to 70 mile radius of their terminal so as to avoid the conflict of not getting drivers home whom do not live within a freight corridor. The best thing to do when researching a carrier is check the lanes of their operation. If it works for you then contact the driver application center. This really pertains to drivers that want to get home; if you want to live in a truck then you are okay.

A note of importance – if you are new to this industry, do not get your hopes up for the days off that you want. You'll need to pay your dues first. On average, if you drive long haul, you get 1 day off for every week that you are out. (Not very enticing is it?) It took me 9 years to finally find a carrier that allows me to have somewhat of a normal life. Of course, it was all about timing for me too. I just happened to catch them before they put an ad in the paper.

Bottom line – take what your recruiter tells you with a grain of salt; they get paid to tell you what you want to hear. Question everything and get their promises in writing. This information will help you find the right carrier and might even make you a happier driver. Who knows, you could be one who lives to drive!!

Hmmmmm???

CHAPTER THREE

Truck Stops

To the four-wheeler truck stops are places to stop for gas and get some munchies. For the city they are located in they are an eyesore. For the trucker it is your home away from home; the "oasis" known as the truck stop. You can count on finding one in every major city and it seems they are all about 50 to 100 miles apart although sometimes they are even a couple hundred miles apart. Statistics show that for every two hundred that close, four hundred are opening. You can pretty much find a truck stop wherever you are unless it is in the middle of nowhere and then what you would come across would be merely a pump and a bathroom with no parking save one or two spots. A truck stop it is not – merely a fuel stop. You will come to know the difference in your travels.

So which is the best truck stop you might ask? While there are thousands of them to choose from, I will focus on the "Big 5"– Flying J, Petro, Travel Centers of America (aka TA's), Pilot and Love's Country Stores. These are the ones you will find in most states and on most routes.

- **Flying J**

    To date, Flying J was merged with Pilot Truck Plaza's; however, when I started writing this guide, Flying J and Pilot Travel Plazas were separate entities so I will follow with that for this summary. While they were the least of my favorite spots to stop at, they do have ample parking, nice restrooms and a restaurant at various locations. The one's to try to avoid, in my opinion, are the Broadway Flying J's. These are the franchise operations and I have not seen one yet that has been pristine. Most are run down, small, contain 2 stalls in the restrooms, and the parking lots are full of holes and ditches. While they maintain the name Flying J, they usually are not maintained the same. This is just a driver's opinion, of course.

- **Petro Stopping Centers/Petro: 2**

Not only was my favorite but recently voted by American truckers as their favorite also. They have the best parking lots, the biggest and cleanest bathrooms (usually two of each), a really good store and best of all the Iron Skillet Restaurant. They've updated their menus and the buffet is worth every penny. The one downfall, in my opinion, is the coffee. The coffee canisters do not keep the coffee hot and it usually goes cold in my thermos after only an hour. Other than that I truly love Petro. Like Flying J, they too have a smaller affiliation – Petro: 2. while they are not a franchise, they are just a smaller version of Petro and the parking is limited as well. I have found that Petro: 2's seem to be in smaller towns rather than in the cities or suburbs.

- **Travel Centers of America (TA)**

I am a little torn on this truck stop. I have been to several TA's and some are really nice while others are really dirty. I know this reflects on management but it can also ruin the reputation as well. At some TA's you'll find restaurants and at others you'll find fast food. On occasion you'll find both at one place. Usually the bathrooms are big, the trucker store is well equipped and the coffee is hot. TA's are usually my second choice when it comes to stopping to fill my thermos. As of summer 2007, the TA organization acquired Petro. Upon reading this news I was a little discouraged that Petro would change for the worse but so far that has not happened. If anything, it might help TA get better. Time will tell, of course.

- **Pilot Travel Centers**

This is my second favorite truck stop and my absolute number one choice for coffee! They have the hottest and best selection. Before the acquisition of Flying J, you could not find a sit down restaurant at Pilot. That is now not the case. More and more Denny's are popping up and they also have subways at the facility. Every now and then you will also find some fast food joints as well. The parking lots vary in size from very large (150+) to very small (25); it just depends on the location. The restrooms are pretty nice and the stores usually have some really great deals.

- **Loves County Store**

This is the fairly new chain among the Big 5 and my least favorite. It seems when my hours are almost up or some weather persists which must take me off the road I most always find Love's at the exit and that's it. I don't like them because they are dirty, the restrooms smell, the store is small the parking is lousy and sometimes they have no parking at all! The coffee's not bad but they don't seem to keep an eye on it when the level gets low.

As of my final entries in this book, Love's has actually improved a great deal and they are even expanding. The lots are nicer, bathrooms are cleaner and coffee has gotten much better. Much has changed in 5 years and it seems for the better.

You might be asking yourself where you might find these truck stops as you are traveling down the interstates. The best thing to do is pick up a National Truck Stop Directory or the Fuel Finder. They both sell for $14.95 and are full of information on services, amenities, scales, etc. These books are life savers and my favorite and most preferred is the Truck Stop Directory.

CHAPTER FOUR

Toll Roads, the East Coast and You

The most nerve racking experience I ever had since I began driving was my first time out to the east coast. If you think the driving experience is the same all over the country you will quickly learn that it is not the case.

I have driven up and down the entire eastern seaboard and I have come to realize that the roads are narrower, save the interstates, the city streets are tighter, people drive crazier and above all else, I have never seen so many toll roads.

On my first ever venture out east, I was not informed of the toll roads and I didn't have the money needed for a big rig so you can imagine the headache this caused. Who would think that Interstate 80 would have tolls on it!

One terrifying incident I encountered was from New Jersey to upstate New York. I guess I had read my map book wrong or I mistook one highway for another and wound up at the toll entrance of the George Washington Bridge into New York City! The booth attendant could see by the look on my face that I had made a huge wrong turn. She actually called up Transit Authority to escort me half way across the bridge to the turnaround point. You could imagine my embarrassment! I have not been back up there since and I hope never to be again.

I also realized when you are on a toll road, the exits are far and few between. If you do get off the toll road, prematurely, it can cost you! Make sure you know where you are going before you leave. This can save you much money and plenty of headaches.

As far as truck stops go, they are very scarce along toll roads. You will not find any of the Big 5 along the way except at the entrance and the exit. What you will find, however, are Travel Plaza's. They are fuel and eating spots along the way. They are placed on the route to avoid having to exit and re-enter and forking out more money than necessary.

My best advice to you, fellow trucker, would be to plan out your east coast venture very carefully and be prepared for anything, as this is a completely different world. Trucks are charged by the weight on these toll roads so have an ample amount of cash on you. The last time I ran these roads the highest I paid was $108.00 and the least amount was $3.80 (this was in Illinois).

CHAPTER FIVE

Canada

As with the east coast, I had not known anything about Canada and I didn't think it would be that much different, except for being a different country. Boy was I wrong! Procedures are much different now than they were in 2000 but I can tell you what to basically expect.

First of all, you will now need a passport to travel into Canada. This is based on Homeland Security rules. You cannot have a felonious record and you must also have your social security number handy and you're ID, of course.

When entering the Port of Entry, expect to be there for a while. My paperwork was not right so it just made my situation that much more complicated. Park in the truck lot and take all the paperwork to the office where it will be verified. Canada uses brokers at the border for loads in and out so be sure your paperwork is issued by a customs broker. Once the authorities have verified your citizenship, truck paperwork, and load information, you will be sent across the street to the customs brokerage offices where you will finalize the rest of your load documents; this can take an hour or longer depending on the line. Once you are done in the brokerage offices, you will be sent back to the Customs office to get your final stamps of approval and then be sent on your way. Oh, and yes, all of this time at the border counts against your hours on duty. You cannot log off duty for any of it.

Canada uses the metric system nationwide. The easy part is your speedometer; it has kilometers on it already. The speed on the highways in Canada is 110km (68mph). You will have to figure out how far your delivery or pick up is based on the conversion of km to miles. This was the hard part. I didn't really do well on the Dewey Decimal System in school. Once you figure it out, you'll do fine. When getting fuel, remember the price posted is for liters. Being in Canada will surely wear you out; the whole math thing.

The change you will receive when buying products with the US dollar, will consist of American and Canadian currency. Not really good as the exchange rate goes due to the fact that the US dollar isn't worth as much in Canada as it used to be. You will definitely take a loss.

All of Canada speaks English except for Quebec. There, all the signs, billboards, papers, and roads are in French. I haven't been there so I am just going by what I have read. I have been to all the other provinces so you will get by just fine there.

Upon leaving Canada, you will go through the same process as you did upon entering. Be sure you state if you bought anything that you are bringing back to the states; Customs will want to see a receipt. Have a good attitude and be pleasant while you are in customs. It doesn't take much for them to search your truck. The smoother you make things for yourself, the smoother it will be getting back into the United States.

CHAPTER SIX

Dispatchers - What You Should Know

In my 20 years of driving, one thing has always remained constant – dispatchers tell you what you want to hear and tell you that they are your best friend. In my opinion, they are all the same and rank right along with recruiters who make things sound better than they are.

Unfortunately, dispatchers have total control of what you do and where you go. They look out for themselves and just consider you a number. This may not describe your dispatcher, but this is how all of mine have been. The trick is to learn how to deal with them. What they don't tell you is that you can "fire" them. I went through four dispatchers before I found one that I could work with. Just remember: they work for **YOU**, you don't work for **THEM**.

If you are new to this industry, keep in mind that dispatchers will sugar coat everything they tell you and will want to keep you out all the time. I have found with the bigger companies if you live in the west you will be running east and vice-versa. When I was involved in a lease purchase (see Chapter 12) I was sent home to Sacramento from Salt Lake City to acquire my belongings and then I had been stuck running between Utah and Massachusetts for the next 3 ½ weeks before I threw up my hands and walked away from my lease and went home.

As a lease driver I had the same options as an owner-operator as far as running where I wanted to, however, my dispatcher never told me this so clearly and I was unaware; I thought I had to run where they saw fit. It's this kind of deceptiveness that dispatchers and fleet managers are known for. Take what they say with a grain of salt and if you have a problem that you can't resolve or are having a difficult time getting home take it up with his or her manager and if it still can't be resolved, then ask for a new dispatcher. Remember – it is your right to do so.

I would recommend, if you are fortunate enough, to get on a regional or dedicated run. You will have the opportunity to make good money and may even be home on a regular basis; let alone, not have to fork out money for toll roads.

CHAPTER SEVEN

Driver Turnover

As I had mentioned in Chapter 2, while you are shopping around for carriers to drive for, be sure to check on the driver turnover rate. This is a really good way to see if the company takes care of drivers; it also shows how stable they are in good and bad economic times. You can find carrier information online.

One of the main reasons for a high driver turnover rate is pay. Drivers are either getting shorted on their load pay, not getting home as they were promised or find a higher paying gig with better benefits and nicer equipment.

I jumped aboard a company with two drivers and they had 5 trucks sitting around. I thought I had found a gold mine as to have my pick of truck but little did I know I would be stuck having to train new drivers coming on, with little or no experience; not what I was told or bargained for by the way. What should have been my first clue that something wasn't quite right was that we were using logs with a different company name on them. Within 3 weeks of coming aboard they shut their doors. I never thought to investigate the driver turnover, let alone the company itself. It's a smart thing to do as it could cost you your job.

CHAPTER EIGHT

Logbooks and CSA

One of the most important documents you'll ever have to sign is the one we call the "logbook." This is the single-most important document you will use during your driving career. This one form can make you or break you; the latter in more ways than one. This is the one thing that the government and trucking industry are at odds over and that regulates how long we can work.

For the past 30+ years, the rules have always been the same – drive 10 hours, sleeper berth for 8 hours, work a total of 15 hours in a day (driving and not driving) and 48 hours off in an 8 day period, or a total of 70 hours in 8 days. As they say, if it doesn't squeak, don't oil it. Too bad if it was recently oiled.

As truck drivers, we are bound by the Federal Motor Carrier Safety Administration, aka FMSCA. They see fit, by their means and the lobbyists, how we as truck drivers need to be regulated. This government agency sets all the hours and equipment requirements set forth in the trucking industry and in my opinion has cause more hurt than not.

While there is still much confusion how the new hours of service are to be followed, I hope I can easily sum them up for you, trucker to trucker. The FMSCA decided it was time to change our hours of service, aka HOS, to appease trucker opposition groups and they have changed greatly.

- **Pre-2005:**

  Driving time   -   10 hours

  On-duty not driving -   5 hours

  Sleeper berth   -   8 hours

Meal breaks   -   2 hours
                                (may be split)

70-hour reset   -   48 hours
                                Consecutively

- **Current HOS:**

Driving time   -   11 hours

On-duty not driving -   3 hours

Sleeper berth   -   10 hours

Meal breaks   -   30 minutes after 8
                                hours coming on
                                duty; does not stop
                                the clock

70-hour Reset   -   34 consecutive
                                hours off duty

- **The main kicker:**

You may only work/drive for 14 hours after coming on duty including the now required 30 minute rest period; which by the way keeps the clock ticking. Yeah, that makes sense.

One misconception is that you cannot work at all after 14 hours; this is not entirely true. You just can't drive after having been on duty for 14 hours. You can still perform other duties but are unable to drive until you have had 10 consecutive hours off or in your sleeper berth or a combo of the two. One thing to take note of, since the FMSCA enacted the two periods of 1 a.m. and 5 a.m., truck stops are getting filled up rather quickly now so later on in the evening into the night it is becoming more difficult to find a place to park. Plan accordingly to save yourself some time and frustration. If you need to park before your hours are up for the day then take advantage of that option. It will enable you to have more hours in the week to get where you need to be. Just because you are allowed to drive 11 hours a day, does not mean you have too. Depending on the type of trailer you are pulling, these hours of service will limit you in your day. I pull a flatbed so my time sitting at shippers and receivers isn't very long so I am able to take advantage of most of my hours. However, if you pull a reefer or van, you will find that you may sitting for hours on end waiting to get loaded/unloaded and this will take away from your clock. Not that you heard it from me but you may have to be creative on your books. This will be a little more difficult if you drive for a carrier with Electronic On Board Recording Devices (EOBRD). These record your time to the minute and some of them will actually shut down your truck once you have hit your limits for the day. Plan your day and your routes carefully because in the end you are responsible for your logbooks and only you. If they are wrong, you are the one who gets the penalty, not your carrier.

Be sure that your logbooks are legible and neat. If you come across a trooper who cannot read your log, that will give him/her reason to go through it. You are required to carry 8 days in your possession- today and the last 7. Please note, you can be cited for speeding 8 days ago based on your logs. Pay attention; log it like you drove it.

Before you begin your day, you will need to fill out your log book. It is pretty much self-explanatory. When filling in your time at stops, **DO NOT** abbreviate. You must spell out the entire name of the city and use the state abbreviation. The one thing you do not want to do is sign your logbook until you have completed your day. The reason being, underneath the line for the signature, is a statement that reads "I certify these entries to be true and correct." If you sign your name before the end of the day, and your logs are not accurate, you will be cited and put out of service for falsifying your logbooks.

As of August 19, 2019, the FMCSA ruled an HOS change to adjust the 34 hour restart and break period as of this publishing. These changes are still in consideration.

CSA:

Compliance, Safety and Accountability

As of 2013, FMSCA has come out with another way to regulate drivers only with this new policy it cannot only hurt you but the carrier you drive for. It is an ever changing environment but I will do my best to try to break it down for you in a way which you can understand.

CSA raises the bar for safety under 7 categories called **BASIC : Behavior Analysis and Safety Improvement Category**

- **UNSAFE DRIVING**

- **HOURS OF SERVICE (HOS) COMPLIANCE**

- **DRIVER FITNESS**

- **CRASH INDICATOR**

- **VEHICLE MAINTENCE**

- **HAZARDOUS MATERIAL (HM) COMPLIANCE**

- **CONTROLLED SUBSTANCES/ALCOHOL**

The BASIC is a scoring system which counts against you and the carrier and will follow you throughout your driving career. The highest percentage, the worst score it is which bring about an investigation. You or the carrier do not want this as some carriers have already been fined and shut down because of multiple violations. One way to keep the carrier from getting a mark on their record is to not get **ANY** violations. I know that is hard to do but it is possible; your carrier will only be penalized if the citation was received while you are driving for them. Only violations within the control of the driver will count toward driver safety profile, e.g., log book violations, speeding, DUI's, etc. The best thing to do is to go by the book and you will be fine.

Do note, however, if the CMV for which you are driving gets a citation and put out of service (not necessarily both), you **AND** the carrier will get poor marks on your safety profile. They claim you are driving the CMV so it is your responsibility to make sure everything is operational; sometimes there are violations you cannot see and at that point it is too late.

CSA focuses primarily on driver enforcement for serious violations such as:

- Driving while disqualified

- Driving without a valid Commercial Driver's License

- Expired Medical Card

- Making a false entry on a medical certificate

- **Committing numerous Hours-of-Service violations**

Do not attempt to try to cheat your employer or the system as with this new system it will only damage you and make it impossible to obtain a job down the road due to your safety profile. Drive smart. Drive legal. It is only in your best interest.

CHAPTER NINE

Scales and the Highway Patrol
Aka Chicken Coops and Bears

I'm sure you've seen them as you blow right on by wondering what that was and if you were supposed to pull in there. You are now looking in your mirrors to see if you have the red and blue lights coming up on you.

Yes, it's happened to all of us; you've just passed an **OPEN** scale and are now worried they are on their way to get you!!

If there is one place out here on the road that can turn a good day into a really **bad** day, it's the truck scale. I cannot count how many times I have had bad experiences at the scales due to a simple line not signed to an annual permit not being updated. The one thing I have learned over my many years of driving is to have your T's crossed, I's dotted and all of your paperwork up to par before entering and crossing over a scale.

The most important piece of paperwork in your truck is the Bill of Lading. This is the form that proves you are to be in possession of the load. **NEVER** cross state lines without a Bill of Lading completely filled out and signed by you **AND** the shipper. If you enter a state without one, you may be looking at multiple fines and possible arrest which in turn will cause your truck to be impounded. This is a situation you want to avoid at all times!

The scales you really want to pay attention to are the ones you come upon when entering a state; these are the POE scales – PORT OF ENTRY. These scale houses are equipped with the sticklers (officers) who are well versed on all state and federal truck laws. If they see something that doesn't look right they will direct you to the inspection area and go over your truck and paperwork with a fine toothed comb. **F. Y. I.** these scales are manned by officers from the state you just left and the state you just entered. If you think you managed to escape a citation from the prior state because you did something on the down-low, think again. They **WILL** cite you in this state. Remember, this POE is considered the state line whether it's on the border or 20 miles in. Don't chance it – stay legal.

When entering these POE's, you will hear over the speaker system to park and bring in your license, medical card, registration and all paperwork. If they want to see your logbook, they will call for it over the speaker. **NEVER** volunteer it!! You should bring it in with you but wait for them to ask for it – if they don't, leave it at that. You can actually get a ticket for a logbook violation 8 days previously if you did your logs wrong and they find it. Technically, if you have a month worth of logs in your possession – only 8 days is required – they can go all the way back and cite you for all the days you were in violation. This is completely legal.

I have noticed over the years that many scales are not manned by state troopers but by the states' DOT Enforcement Division. Do not be fooled – these personnel can write the same citation as a state trooper. In fact, they are trained in the laws more than a trooper. My advice is to treat them just as you would a state trooper, give them respect and they will respect you back most of the time. You will run into a few of them who have it out for truckers and it has actually gotten to the point of being harassment if you want to know the truth. I always try to go in with a smile and have answers to their questions and the result is always positive. If you just be professional you should be in and out of there in a few minutes.

There is one curious thing I have discovered over the last few years – it has been said that the scales in front of you do not know when you entered the state behind you so if you have to fudge your logbook, no problem, they'll never know. This just is not the case anymore. The states that I am aware of doing this are Oregon, Washington, Utah, Colorado and Arizona. I learned the hard way of course. I left Oregon state a half hour too early, entered Washington POE and was shut down for 10 hours and received a hefty fine for it of course. Don't think they don't know; nine out of ten, they DO!!!!

CHAPTER TEN

Trailers - Types and Hassles

While there are many types of trailers being pulled down the road, I will focus on the ones I have pulled over the years. These include the most common type of trailer and I can guarantee you have pulled or are currently pulling one of these right now. Despite popular belief, you do not drive a "semi"; you pull a semi. The **trailer** is the semi.

- **Vans**

  This is basically a box on wheels. They range from 45 to 53 feet long. They are primarily used for non-perishable products. The floors are made of wood and are cleaned easily by the push of a broom.

- **Reefers (Refrigerated)**

These trailers are just a van; however, they are a freezer on wheels. They have a refrigeration unit on the nose and the floors are primarily full aluminum. These units have a temperature indicator on the nose of the trailer visible from your mirror. It indicates if the unit is operational by two colors – red and green. If it is red, stop and check the unit. If it is green you are good to go. The hassles with this trailer are that you must constantly keep it clean and fueled. Most of the products for this trailer are perishable and shippers will not load you if you have a dirty floor. Just keep in mind you .have a fuel tank on this trailer; a good rule is to fuel this one up when you are filling your tractor. You will never run out of fuel and will not lose the product.

- **Container Chassis**

These trailers are fairly simple but you can have problems with them. The sizes of chassis are 20, 40, 45, 48 and 53 feet. Unless you drive for a company that owns their own chassis, you will be pulling some pretty beat up equipment. You can imagine the wear on them as they are staged at ocean ports and hauled by a multitude of drivers. The most common failure you will experience with these trailers is the tires and lights. The tires on these are commonly recaps and the lights are hardly checked. The most important device on these trailers is the container locks. Be sure these are working properly or you can lose the container from the trailer.

Pulling a 40, 45 and 53 foot container is no different than any other trailer. The 20-footer, however, is the one you must be extra careful with when loaded. These will easily tip over if you turn too quickly as there is quite a bit of weight put in them.

- **Car Trailers**

While pulling these trailers, you definitely have to know what you are doing. There are two types of car trailers – open and enclosed. You should be well trained when pulling these trailers in order not to cause damage to the cars on them. Most of them do not have any kind of anti-slip on them so loading them in the snow can create a challenge. This is where the enclosed trailers come in handy; albeit, you lose maneuvering room due to the box around the trailer frame. Although it is possible to be overweight on one of these trailers, it does not happen too often. I pulled one for a 3 year period and never had and overweight ticket. You need to be careful as to where you put the heavier vehicles. Usually you put smaller and lighter cars on top and on the end and heavier ones in the middle and on the bottom. These trailers are pretty easy to deal with other than the clearance underneath. Be sure not to attempt a U-turn on a crowned road as the clearance is a matter of inches.

- **Flatbeds**

These trailers are vans minus the walls and roof and sit about 5 feet off the ground which limits your load height capability. There are two types of flatbeds –regular and extendable. The lengths are 20, 30, 40, 45, 48 and 53 foot. A step deck is a flatbed trailer but the usual terminology for them is step-deck as you have to "step" up to the upper deck. You are able to load higher on these trailers as they are only 3 feet off the ground and not 5 feet. The load has a lower center of gravity so the likelihood of it tipping over is pretty rare. The downside of pulling any type of flatbed trailer, in most cases than not, is that in winter you will have to cover your loads with tarps. This can be dangerous due to the fact you are on top of the load and you must make slow moves and know where your feet are as you can easily move over too much one way and fall off the load. Other than the danger factor involved, flatbeds and step-decks are great to pull and it also gives you a certain level of respect out here due to the driver having to brave the elements for their load. Pulling these trailers also tends to pay more than the average van or reefer trailer.

- **RGN (Removable Goose Neck)**

  These are what you call a specialized trailer. The trick with these is that they unhook behind the fifth-wheel plate and are primarily used for rolling stock. These trailers also have a ground clearance of just a few inches and can carry much more weight than a step-deck and flatbed.

- **Double Drops**

  These trailers are called double drops due to the 5 foot upper deck in the front, the 5 foot upper deck in the rear and a lower deck of about 25-35 feet just a few inches off the ground. Most of the loads for these trailers are really tall and putting them on these keeps you within legal limits.

- **Lowboy or Lowbed**

  This trailer is primarily used for heavy equipment. It sits about 6 inches off the ground and contains many tires – about 20 of them; 10 per axle.

- **Landoll**

  I have been pulling this type of trailer for 14 years and I love it. They range in length from 30 feet to 53 feet. They lift up just behind the fifth-wheel and are considered a rolling loading ramp as you can pretty much load it anywhere. They contain a winch and remote control and look like a step-deck. The only downfall is that they are heavy and on my 35 ton trailer my max weight is 41,780 pounds. What makes them heavy is the hydraulic ram which runs down the center of the trailer to run the rear axle assembly forward for loading. These trailers, too, sit like a step deck- 3 feet off the ground.

- **Tanker/Bulk**

  As it states, this is a rolling tank. I have never pulled one before but word has it when pulling one you can feel the load swashing around. You should be just as careful with one of these as you would with a 20 foot container chassis.

After pulling a trailer for a while, you will grow used to how it rides and the hassles of it. All in all, you become so familiar with it; it tends to become shorter and quite easy to pull around. Just remember this important note – a good driver pulls a trailer – not drag a trailer.

Chapter Eleven

Four wheelers Suck!

In this industry we deal with all sorts of hassles but none will compare to those evil things we truckers like to call "the four-wheeler." Every dangerous thing you can think of, a four-wheeler will cause it; every accident you can imagine yourself being in, a four-wheeler probably caused it; every stupid maneuver you've ever seen done, a four-wheeler has or is currently doing it.

One advantage that the trucking industry can use is a push to the motor vehicle departments to incorporate written instruction for new drivers and renewing drivers on the do's and don'ts of driving near or next to big rigs. From what I've seen already, California (my home state) has implemented such instruction, however, it could be a little more in depth. People just do not know how to drive when it comes to sharing the road with big trucks. Here are just a few things you should be aware of:

- When you activate your turn signal, it WILL become a magnet for cars. That four-wheeler you saw a half mile behind you when you activated your turn signal is now alongside you hovering.

- You swore you saw that car behind you a second ago, yet it did not pass. This is because it is riding the draft about two feet from the rear of your trailer.

- When entering a highway, a four-wheeler will ride up alongside you until you are the one to back off. As of late, I acquired information about this and was told that it is not our responsibility, as a big rig driver, to let the merging traffic in our lane. You can, and will, be cited for improper lane usage. It is called merging for a reason.

- When in a traffic back-up due to a lane closure, four-wheelers will wait until the lane is completely blocked with cones before moving over and will expect you to let them in.

- Four-wheelers will **ALWAYS ride** alongside your blind side on the right. They will only move when they see your signal and then they will bolt out in front of you. This happens on a regular basis.

- No matter the lack of room in front of you on highways, four-wheelers will **ALWAYS zoom** past you and squeeze in.

Be aware of these at all times for it will save you the headache of rear end accident. You see, the four-wheeler will just assume that you will let it in but this is not always the case.

These are just a few examples of what it is like to share the road with four-wheelers. Statistics show that 90% of all auto-big rig accidents are caused by four-wheelers while 70% of fatalities involving big rigs are caused by four-wheelers. The bottom line is - - **ALL THOSE CARS AROUND YOU ON HIGHWAYS AND CITY STREETS REALLY HAVE NO IDEA HOW TO SHARE THE ROAD WITH BIG TRUCKS.**

It comes down to you not only watching out for yourself, but all those around you too. It is a big responsibility, I know, but someone has to be the professional.

CHAPTER TWELVE

Lease - Purchase
The Truth Behind the Lie

This is one subject I am very familiar with as I was involved in a lease-purchase for only 30 days however; I gained a lifetime of wisdom on the subject matter.

Many companies today are hyping about a lease-purchase as a way to enter the industry through them. While this sounds like an appealing idea, it is also a bad one. Sure, it looks good on paper but in the end the numbers don't make any sense and it becomes a headache you do not want.

The following is my experience:

There I was, a company driver in need of something more. I didn't know what I was looking for until I came across an ad that I thought would change my life forever. It changed it alright, but at the time certainly not for the better. The offer sounded really good but hidden behind it were the lies that I would not discover until I was in over my head.

Once I applied, it took about two weeks to finalize my application. I asked all the pertinent questions and the situation sounded very promising. I gave my notice to my current employer and I was on a plane bound for Salt Lake City.

Upon arrival, I checked in at the company and began a two week orientation.There, the focus was on how to make money as a lease-operator and the do's and don'ts of running a successful business. The final stage of the orientation was the contract signing. This had to be the longest contract I had ever seen before. The wording was your typical contract jargon and half of it didn't really make any sense. When reviewing the contract, I had asked if I could have my attorney look it over and was told I could take it with me but only after I signed and committed to it first; this should have been the first clue that something was not right. After signing the contract (at this point I was feeling very uneasy), I met with the accounting department and went over all of the financials. Upon completion of the contract process, it was time to select my "new" truck.

What I thought would be an assortment of trucks to choose from, it turned out to be a very minimal choice; seven to be exact. I was told that more would be coming in but not for another week. My contract signed, I had to choose a truck as my first week's truck payment had been waived so I needed to get myself on the road to make money so I could stay a week ahead of the game. So I picked my truck, a 2002 Freightliner XL with 163,000 miles on it and it seemed new enough as these miles aren't even break-in miles for a tractor. I came to find out $1000.00 later that this truck had problems. I received my truck book e.g., permits, licensing, insurance, etc., and was awaiting my plates – due at the facility in a couple of hours. That couple of hours turned into a half day and that half day turned into 2 weeks; this should have been my second clue as to something not being right. The other lease-operators had already left the yard with their first loads and free week and there I was still waiting for my plates. Did the company give me another free week due to their incompetence? No they did not!!! Turns out the plates were lost between the dealership and the terminal and new ones had to be ordered. At this point I was ready to say to hell with all of this.

So my plates finally came in and now I needed a load. I was told I would have a load on Friday, two days from now. Really? Talk about a waste of two weeks. I finally got my load and it took me back out to California where I was able to get home, pick up my personal affects and make some money. (Fat Chance!)

I gave my wife, pregnant at the time, a kiss goodbye and I headed out to Boston. I proceeded to run from Utah to Massachusetts over the next 3 weeks not once getting home to Sacramento. The company failed to tell me that I was able to pick and choose loads so I felt compelled to have to take what they gave me. My income for the last 3 **weeks – $120.00**!! That's right; this is all I made for almost the month that I had this truck. My whole world had just caved in on me and I realized that I made the worst decision of my whole working life!! The wool had just been pulled over my head.

Upon returning to the yard in Salt Lake City, I demanded to know if these people made a living destroying peoples' lives with their lies and deceit. It got to the point that I had to be escorted out of the building while waiting for my cab to take me to the bus depot. In the end, here is how things turned out for me:

- My truck made a gross income of $8365.00 for 30 days. My cut – **$120.00!**

- Multiple hidden charges I was never aware of.

- Truck broke down multiple times and the so-called warranty I was supposed to have had on it covered nothing. I paid over $1000.00 out of pocket.

- I was facing a repossession of my vehicle and electricity shut off at home.

- Wife was at home, pregnant, with no money coming in.

When I questioned the carrier about where all the money from the truck went, I was told that it went into my escrow fund, in addition to the truck charges, i.e., payments, insurance, licensing, taxes, fuel, etc. I came to find out I was being charged many hidden costs, one of them being for the satellite communications system they have installed in the trucks. It was quite shocking how defensive these people became when I questioned them on where they were putting my money.

While I mentioned my first two clues as to why this was probably not a good idea to get into, my third and biggest clue should have been the fact the while still in the orientation process, **50** drivers had already turned in their lease trucks; and that was just THAT week! Like they say, hindsight is 20 - 20. In the end, I am very glad I got out of this thing and went home.

So what is the lesson here? For starters, do not jump into any contract until you research all the information first. If you are working to be in a lease-purchase plan, do not have a home you'll have to maintain as you won't make any money to sustain it; you're better off living in your truck. The big kicker is that when you come to the end of the lease purchase, do not believe the dollar buyout; this final payment is usually a balloon payment that is way too high. It's as though you just paid for the tractor you are driving TWICE! The most important lesson I learned through this experience is that a lease driver is basically a glorified company driver. You have the benefits of an owner-operator but you do not have the income of an owner-operator and all the headaches of a bad idea.

It is in my opinion that you are better off being a company driver. You will definitely make more money.

CHAPTER THIRTEEN

Trucker Talk
AKA CB LINGO

Think back to when you were a kid and you would see big trucks cruising down the road and the driver was talking on that big radio. You would wonder to yourself who he was talking to and what he was saying.

The language he was speaking is what is known as "trucker talk" or simply put – CB Jive. While the language has changed course over the last 3 decades it has still stuck to the basic terms with a few that are seldom or rarely used but nonetheless, are still used.

Not only will I introduce you to our language, but I will also list for you the universal 10-Codes that are used by all agencies and sometimes heard on the CB radio.

RADIO 10 CODES

- 10-1   Receiving Poorly
- 10-2   Receiving Well
- 10-3   Stop Transmitting
- 10-4   OK; Message Received
- 10-5   Relay Message
- 10-6   Busy; Stand By
- 10-7   Out Of Service
- 10-8   In Service
- 10-9   Repeat Message
- 10-10   Transmission Completed;
                  Standing By; At home
- 10-11   Talking Too Rapidly
- 10-12   Visitors Present
- 10-13   Advise Weather/Road
                  Conditions
- 10-16   Make Pick Up At......
- 10-17   Urgent Business
- 10-18   Anything Pending
- 10-19   Return To Base

- 10-20   What's Your Location
- 10-21   Call By Landline
- 10-22   Report In Person
- 10-23   Stand By
- 10-24   Completed Last Assignment
- 10-25   Make Contact With.....
- 10-26   Disregard Last Transmission
- 10-27   Moving to Channel......
- 10-28   Identify Your Station
- 10-30   Does Not Conform To FCC Regs
- 10-32   Radio Check
- 10-33   Accident
- 10-34   Trouble At This Station, Send Help
- 10-35   Confidential Information
- 10-36   Time Check
- 10-37   Wrecker Needed
- 10-38   Ambulance Needed
- 10-39   Message Relayed
- 10-41   Tune To Different Channel
- 10-42   I Agree; Copy

- 10-43   Traffic Jam
- 10-44   Message Alert
- 10-45   All Units Report
- 10-49   In Route
- 10-50   Break Channel
- 10-62   Not Clear; Use Landline
- 10-65   Standing By
- 10-70   Fire
- 10-73   Speed Trap
- 10-75   Causing Interference
- 10-77   Negative Contact
- 10-84   My Phone Number
- 10-85   My Address Is......
- 10-91   Get Closer To Mic
- 10-97   Arrived On Scene
- 10-98   All Clear
- 10-99   In Tow; Unit Rolling
- 10-100   Restroom Break

TRUCKER TALK AKA CB LINGO

<u>A</u>

ATTIC: CB Channel 40

ANT EATER: Kenworth T600 Tractor

AFFIRMATIVE: Yes; 10-4

ALLIGATOR: Chunk of big truck tire on the road

<u>B</u>

BACK DOOR: Behind you; to the rear

BACK IT DOWN: Reduce Speed

BACK ROW: Rear parking in truck stop

BAMBI: A deer, alive or dead, on or near road

BAND-AID BOX: An ambulance

BAREFOOT: Going over mountain pass without chains

BAREFOOT CB: Out of box radio; factory

BEAR: Generic term for law enforcement officer

BEAR BAIT: Big truck or four-wheeler speeding

BEAR BITE: A speeding ticket

BEAR CAVE: Police station or Highway Patrol HQ

BEAR IN THE AIR: Law enforcement airplane or chopper

BEAR PLANE: Same as above

BEAR IN THE BUSHES: Police are hiding

BEDBUGGERS: Moving companies of household goods

BENDER-N-FENDER: Fender bender

BETTER HALF: A drivers' spouse

BIG ROAD: An interstate highway

BIG TRUCK: A tractor-trailer

BIRD DOG: Radar detector

BLACK EYE: Burnt out headlight

BLUE LIGHT SPECIAL: Cops with lights flashing

BOBTAIL: Running without a trailer

BLINKER FLUID: Term used to tell driver to turn off signal

BROWN PAPER BAG: Brown unmarked police vehicle

BLACK WATER: Coffee

BOULEVARD: Interstate

BREAK: Proper way to gain access to busy channel

BRAKE CHECK: Traffic stopped or slowing

BREAKING UP: Not coming in clear on radio

BRUSH YOUR TEETH AND COMB YOUR HAIR: Coming up on police with radar gun.

BUBBLE GUM MACHINE: Police with emergency lights on

BULL HAULER: Livestock trailer

BUMPER STICKER: Car riding too close to your trailer

BUSTER BROWN: UPS truck/driver

C

CABBAGE PATCH: A long steep downgrade on 1-84 in Eastern Oregon

CARE BEAR: Law Enforcement in a construction zone

CASH REGISTER: Toll booth

CAR-B-QUE: Car fire

CHICKEN LIGHTS: Extra lights on truck and trailer

CHICKEN COOP: State Weigh Stations

CHECKING GROUND PRESSURE: Scales open; rolling trucks through

CITY KITTY: Female city police officer

C.O.E.: A cab over tractor

COME BACK: A call to anyone listening "Thanks for the comeback......Where is the truck stop?"

COME ON: A call directed to a certain person "Got your ears on Johnny, come on?"

COMIC BOOK: A log book

COMMERCIAL OR COMMERCIAL GIRL: A prostitute

COMEDIAN: A highway center median strip

CONVENTIONAL: A tractor with a hood as opposed to a C.O.E.

CONVOY: A group of trucks traveling very close together front to rear

COPY: Transmission received, via CB

COOP: see **CHICKEN COOP**

CHRISTMAS LIGHTS: Emergency lights on an official vehicle

COUNTY MOUNTY: A sheriff's deputy

COVERED WAGON: Gravel trailer with a tarp

CROTCH ROCKET: A motorcycle

<u>D</u>

DAY CARE BEAR: Plain clothes officer

DEAD HEAD: Empty miles; rarely pays well

DESTRUCTION ZONE: Construction zone

DOG/GREY DOG: Greyhound bus

DOUBLE-NICKLE: 55 M.P.H. Speed limit

DOUBLES: Double semi-trailers; aka wiggle wagons, widow makers and pups.

DO WHAT?: Did not copy, please repeat. Also Radio Code 10-9

DRAGGIN' FLY: A truck climbing up a hill very slowly and flying down the other side

DRAGGIN' WAGON: A wrecker or tow truck
DRIVER: A term for truck drivers on CB if unaware of handle name; rarely do we say "Trucker"

DRIVER AWARD: A ticket

DRY BOX: A freight trailer; also called a van

DRESS FOR SALE: A prostitute

DRAWING LINES: Filling out log book

DUNNAGE: 8 X 4 planks of wood for loading flatbeds and step decks

E

EARS: CB antennas

EVIL KNIEVEL: A motorcycle cop

EYEBALL(ING): Headlight; to view something

F

FLAPPERS: CB antennas

FLIPSIDE: Return trip "see you on the flipside"

FOUR-WHEELER: A vehicle with four wheels

FULL GROWN: Highway Patrol cruiser

FRONT DOOR: In front of you; lead truck in a convoy

FEED THE BEARS: To pay a ticket or fine

FLATBED: A flatbed trailer; also referred to as a skateboard

FLATBED ROW: An area in truck stop where flatbeds park; usually in the back 40 because they carry wide loads

FLIP-FLOP: A U-turn

FREIGHTSHAKER: Commonly known as a Freightliner tractor

FURNITURE WRECKERS: Moving companies

G

GEARJAMMER: A truck driver

GEARSLAMMER: A speeding truck driver

GOOD BUDDY: Used to mean friend. Now it is a negative term referring to a homosexual

GO JUICE: Diesel fuel

GOOD NEIGHBOR: Friend; replaced **GOOD BUDDY**

GOOD OL' DAYS: Refers to the time when trucking was profitable for drivers; before deregulation in 1980

GOT YER EARS ON?: When looking for a specific person on the CB

GET ON-GET OFF RAMP: Refers to interstate and highway on and off ramps

GRANNY LANE: The right lane, or slow lane, on an interstate or highway

GRASS: The center median strip; see **COMEDIAN**

GREASY: Icy or slippery road

GREASY SIDE UP: A car or truck lying on its top

GROUND PRESSURE: Truck weight

GROSSED OUT: Term used for maximum allowable weight for a truck and trailer without a special permit i.e., 80,000 pounds

GUMBALL MACHINE: Lights on top of police cruiser; see **CHRISTMAS LIGHTS**

GRAPEVINE: Mountain pass in Southern California on the north-south route of Interstate 5

H

HAMMER LANE: Far left lane of interstate; fast lane

HIGH DOLLAR LANE: See **HAMMER LANE;** trucks usually receive much steeper fines for using this lane

HAMMER DOWN: Speed up

HAMSTER: A slow moving, low horsepower truck climbing a steep grade

HANDLE: A distinctive name a driver uses on the CB; "What's your handle driver? This here is Mama Bear"

HAPPY HAPPY: A happy new year wish

HOLLAR: Call me on the CB when you get a chance

HOLLYWEIRD: Hollywood, California

HOW 'BOUT IT: Used to make contact with someone on CB "How 'bout it, need some local info"

HOME 20: Your place of residence

HAULIN' DISPATCHER BRAINS: Pulling an empty trailer; pays very little, if at all

HOOD ORNAMENT: A car that speeds up to get around you and then slows way down one in front of you

HOOK: Tow truck; see **DRAGGIN' WAGON**

HAIR DRYER: A radar gun

I

IN THE BIG HOLE: In top gear

IDIOT BOX: Television

INVITATIONS: Traffic and/or speeding tickets; see **DRIVER AWARD**

IRON: Snow chains

J

JEWELRY: Tire chains; see **IRON**

JACKPOT: When emergency lights are engaged on unit

K

KW/K-DUB: A Kenworth tractor

KEY UP: Talk on the CB microphone

KIDDIE CAR: A school bus

KOJACK WITH A KODAK: A law enforcement officer using a radar gun

L

LINEAR: An illegal CB signal booster

LEFT COAST: The west coast

LOCAL INFO: A radio call for local directions

LOG BOOK: Book truckers use to record duty status

LAND LINE: A hard wired phone

LEGAL BEAGLE: A driver who operates by the letter of the law

LOLLIPOP: A mile-marker post on a highway or interstate

LOT LIZARD: A truck stop prostitute; see **COMMERCIAL; DRESS FOR SALE**

LUMPER: A person hired to load/unload product from a trailer

<u>M</u>

MEAT WAGON: Ambulance

MERRY MERRY: A Merry Christmas greeting

MOTION LOTION: Fuel; see **GO JUICE**

MILE MARKER: Highway mile number post; see **LOLLIPOP**

MONSTER LANE: Passing lane; see **HAMMER LANE; HIGH DOLLAR LANE**

<u>N</u>

NEGATIVE: No; the term **NEGATORY** is also used

NEIGHBOR: Other truck drivers

NO DOUBT: I know you're right

<u>O</u>

ONE WAY CAMPER: An ambulance; see **MEAT WAGON**

OCTOPUS: A term referring to a car hauler

<u>P</u>

PARKING LOT: A car hauler; see **OCTOPUS**

PETE: A Peterbilt tractor

PICKEM-UP TRUCK: A pickup truck

PAY THE WATER BILL: Restroom break

PICKLE PARK: Rest area

PLAIN WHITE WRAPPER: An unmarked, white police car

PUMPKIN: A Schneider National Carriers truck

POWER UP: Go fast; step on it

PREESHAYDIT: Thank you very much

R

RADIO: A CB

RADIO CHECK: A call to check the operation of a CB

RAKE THE LEAVES: The rear truck in a convoy looking for BEARS

RATCHET JAW: Person on CB who won't stop talking

READING THE MAIL: Listening to the CB without talking

REEFER: Refrigerated semi-trailer

ROACH COACH: A meal truck

ROAD PIZZA: Road kill

ROGER: Yes, or Okay

ROLLER SKATE: Car; **FOUR-WHEELER**

RUNNING OUT OF REAL ESTATE: A lane closure or merging lane ending

RUNNING YOU ACROSS: Open scale weighing quickly

ROLLING REFINERY: Fuel truck

REAL ESTATE: Traffic lane

<u>S</u>

SALT SHAKER: A snow plow

SAND BOX: A gravel truck

SANDWICH LANE: The middle lane on a 3 lane highway

SESAME STREET: CB channel 19

SHAKE THE TREES: The lead truck in a convoy looking out for **BEARS**

SHAKY SIDE: The West Coast; **LEFT COAST**

STAGE STOP: Truck stop

SHORT SHORT: A short amount of time

SHE BEAR: A female cop; **CITY KITTY**

SHINY SIDE UP: A safe trip wish to other drivers

SHUTDOWN: A driver/truck put out of service by DOT

SINGLE SCREW: One drive axle

SKATEBOARD: A step deck semi-trailer

SKIP: Long range radio signal

SMOKEY: Law enforcement officer: also known as **SMOKEY BEAR**

SMOKIN' THE BRAKES: Brakes getting hot

SHOOTIN' YA IN THE BACK: A hidden cop using a radar gun on you after you pass.

STAND ON IT: Accelerate quickly; see also **HAMMER DOWN**

STAGECOACH: A tour bus

SWINGING DOOR POLICY: Scales opening and closing

T

TAKING PICTURES: A cop using a radar gun; see also **KOJACK WITH A KODAK**

TALL GEARS: A fast truck

THERMOS BOTTLE: A tanker truck hauling chemicals under pressure

THROWING IRON: Putting on chains

TIRE CHALKIN': Using the side of the truck between cab and trailer as restroom

TOOTHPICKS: Lumber

TURKEY DAY: Thanksgiving

TWO-WHEELER: A motorcycle

TWIN SCREWS: Two drive axles

W

WIGGLE WAGON: A truck pulling doubles/triples

WALKED ON YA: Someone keyed up on you during transmission; did not copy what you said.

WALL TO WALL: A loud and clear radio transmission; also describes heavy police coverage

WALLY WORLD: A Walmart truck

WAGON: A semi-trailer

WATERIN' THE TIRES: Using the space between cab and trailer for restroom; see also **TIRE CHALKIN'**

YARD STICK: Mile marker

YAPPER: Someone who won't stop talking

Z

ZIPPER: Lane divider lines on highways and interstates

So that pretty much covers the CB Lingo. You will probably hear other terms that I haven't listed and that is due to new ones popping up almost every day. The list I have given at least gives you an idea of what you're hearing and you can go from there.

Now the big question – what channel of the 40 available do you use? Well, it all depends on where you are. The basic rule states that if you are running east and west; tune your radio to channel 19; north and south, channel 17. It is a rule changer however, when you are running in California.

Let's first focus on Northern California. Specifically north of Highway 46 in Lost Hills, CA in Fresno County on Interstate 5 northbound.

From this point north to the Oregon border the channel you run is 17. On Interstate 80 from San Francisco to the Nevada border, you run both 17 and 19; the traffic on these channels is heavy as some locals use both of them due to the crowded airwaves. On Highway 99 use channel 17; on Highway 50, channel 19.

Southern California, on Interstate 5 at Highway 46 heading south, you will use channel 15. Why it changes, I do not know as it has been this way as long as I have been driving.

Once you climb over the mountain pass known as the Grapevine that is when the channels go all different. The rule of thumb is this:

> When running to and in southern California all freeways south and east of Interstate 5 run channel 15. All freeways north and west of Interstate 5 run channel 17. The freeways that always run channel 19 are Interstate 15, Interstate 215, Interstate 210, Interstate 10, Interstate 710, Interstate 605, Interstate 405, Highway 57, 60 and 91. Highway 101, from Interstate 5, north, runs channel 17.

Despite everything you've come to believe about interstates, I do not know why the above mentioned routes are called interstates as they are only regional roads. That one will always keep me pondered.

A final note, despite popular belief, channel 9, the emergency channel, is hardly ever monitored. You will be better off using your phone or getting a driver on the CB to call help for you. I know this from experience. Channel 9 was worthless. I got a driver on 17 and an ambulance arrived.

CHAPTER FOURTEEN

PROFESSIONALISM AND COURTESY

There was a time when this industry had those two words melded into it, 20 years ago to be exact; when I was a rookie. I was trained by an "old timer" who took pride in driving a truck. Everything I was taught I took to heart and I continue to use it today. Trucking used to be a solid brotherhood but anymore that is not the case. As I see it, here are some of my reasons as to why.

- Over the years, there has been a huge growth of truck schools. This is not a bad thing per se, except they are not teaching the comradery; that can't be learned. In turn it is every man for himself.

- The problem with many of these truck schools is that they are owned and operated by the major truck companies and the students are trained by company standards; not the trucking standards as a whole. I was with one company who trained their drivers and most were out of jail work programs that were hired on as part of their plea agreement. They were gang bangers and wore the clothes as such. Not very professional and courteous in my book.

- Many foreigners are coming to America and don't speak the language; which is very odd to me that they are driving a truck and it is my understanding that one must be able read and write English fluently to hold a CDL.

- Many of the old timers have already or are currently retiring. They are the ones who were teaching pride in this industry.

- A high percentage of drivers out here are driving to live and are just looking out for themselves.

It is up to you, the driver, to display the courtesy and professionalism that this industry is losing. It is up to you to show the motoring public that truck drivers are not just in the way out here on the road.

CHAPTER FIFTEEN

Mishaps You Can Learn From

At one time or another, we've all had bad days at work that you will never live down; it's all a part of working. However, in the trucking industry, these bad days are magnified. The following are some of the mishaps that I've had which are the most memorable and have definitely learned from. Maybe you'll learn from them too; or at least learn NOT to do them!

- July 1997: The first day on the job in a four-car hauler while leaving the yard, I ran over a suspension spring and it got lodged really tight between the duals. It took 3 hours to get it out.

- July 1999: While unloading my four-car hauler, I decided that I would take a short cut and laid the wrong way on the bed to take the J-hooks off of the axle. When I was trying to get up, I lost my balance, rolled off the bed, and landed face down on the concrete with my right hand under me. I shattered my wrist and was on workers comp for 8 months.

- Summer 1998: A car on my deck came loose from the cable and when the light turned green, I moved forward and the car rolled backwards on top of the car I was towing.

- March 2000: While delivering a load to a home improvement store, I pulled the load ropes off and sliding glass doors fell on me, pinning me against the wall of the trailer. It caused me to suffer from an acute shoulder separation and I was on workers comp for 12 months.

- Spring 2001: While stowing my dunnage under the trailer, the bungee cord used to wrap it snapped and sent the hook flying into my face hitting my glass lenses on my sunglasses. My trainer took me to the hospital for an eye washout. Although I was wearing sunglasses, they saved my eyes.

- Summer 2001: While loading a container on my trailer, I noticed it wasn't coming up straight. Instead of unloading it and getting it right, I thought I would use an old trick and use the binder bar to move it over. Well ... that didn't work. I was pulling on the bar and when it slipped, it popped me square in the forehead. I drove myself home first to show my wife what I had done and after she chewed me out, she asked me why I came home first instead of going to the hospital. I discovered the best way to get in ER really fast is to have blood pouring down my face!

- Summer 2003: I was on a military base loading a bull dozer on the downslope of a hill. The weight of the dozer caused the truck to jump the chalks and started barreling down the hill; all the while I was ON the trailer guiding the loader on. When I realized what was happening, I jumped off the trailer and watched my truck, trailer, dozer and the guy on it roll down the hill 100 yards and jackknife at the bottom when it hit a stack of plywood. The only damage caused to the tractor was a small hole in the condenser. To teach me a lesson about NOT loading downhill, I was put on yard duty for 2 weeks. The loading ramp at the base – made out of dirt!!

- Summer 2007: I was carrying a permit load to Cole Washington on a permit that the WSDOT issued me. I came into Spokane Washington on my route when I began to go under a railroad trestle which had a vertical clearance of 14' 4"; my load was 14' 3". Apparently, the DOT had repaved the road and did not inform the WSDOT. I called 911 asking for police assistance and when the officer arrived he was left laughing and scratching his head! In the end, I managed to back out from under the trestle a half mile, escorted by the officer for 2 miles on a non-permitted route and 2 miles back to my regular route on the other side of the trestle. Fortunately all this happened at 2:30 in the morning.

- Fall 2007: While in Houston Texas at a stop light, a four-wheeler came up alongside me on the right just as the light was turning green. I did not know the car was there until I grabbed second gear and saw it shoot out of the right side of me onto the street to my right. I stopped but the car kept going. My damage – a lug nut cover. I could only imagine what was done to the four-wheeler!

- Oct 2013: While operating a forklift to load light towers onto my trailer I hit a pothole too fast and braked too hard. Steel slides on steel – the light tower fell to the ground on its side.

- Mar 2014: While moving electric pallet jacks around on my trailer, one got away from me and fell off the side. It is REALLY hard to hold up 1200 pounds all by yourself. My employer wound up having to buy that one.

- Summer 2014: While disconnecting a drive line on a motor home so I could tow it 177 miles back to the yard, I lost hold of it and it fell on the tip of my left ring finger. The doctor told me that had I not had on my leather gloves, I would have lost the fingertip. ALWAVS wear gloves!!

- March 2015: As fork-lift was rolling off my trailer I decided to get behind it to stop it until I realized what I was doing. I jumped out of the way and let it drop. The image of being crushed remained in my head for 8 months.

While there have been many other mishaps that have occurred during the years of trucking, these are ones that sit with me the most. If there is anything I have learned – the most important is never expect ANYTHING and always expect EVERYTHING. Take it from me; you will be able to compose your own list of mishaps if you are driving a truck. It is inevitable that stuff will happen. It is the nature of the beast.

CHAPTER SIXTEEN

The Great US of A & Trucker Pride

When I was younger, I had never realized that there was a much bigger country out there just past my front door. When I saw a big truck for the first time, it seemed to me to be alive. I was fascinated by them and always wondered what it would be like to just get inside of one. Now here I am, a grown man with 20 years of driving experience under my belt and over a million and a half miles and I wouldn't change a thing.

As I mentioned at the beginning of this Guide, it is the drive that keeps me going; the passion of hitting the open, road and seeing where it takes me. The best part of it is experiencing the beauty of this great country and the endless changing scenery along the asphalt, as well as the freedom of being out on the open road and not stuck in an office doing the same thing day in and day out; every day it is something different when driving a truck.

Over the years I have had many drivers tell me how much they hate what they're doing. It's this attitude that gives us truckers a bad rap. When you do not like what you are doing it shows in the daily aspect of the work you do – aggressive driving, cutting off other drivers in traffic, loads not secured properly, etc.

The most important aspect of trucking is that in order to be a safe, cautious and a professional driver you must have pride in what you do. Remember this, you put in all the footwork, e.g., truck driving school, tuition and time to get where you are; you made the choice to be a truck driver. Be proud of what you are doing!

Truckers were once known as the Knights of the Road.If enough of us start taking pride in what we do, then we can bring the honor back into this industry. As far as I am concerned, being a truck driver is not just what I do – it's who I am.